COMPREHENSION COLLECTION

LEVEL 6

A Remedia Publication

Written by Anne Sattler

Illustrated by Danny Beck

ISBN #1-56175-399-8

©Remedia Publications. All rights reserved. Printed in the United States of America. The purchase of this book entitles the individual teacher to reproduce copies for classroom use only. The reproduction of any part for an entire school or school system or for commercial use is strictly prohibited.

REMEDIA PUBLICATIONS   10135 E. VIA LINDA, #D124   SCOTTSDALE, AZ 85258
Toll Free 1-800-826-4740   FAX 602-661-9901

ANSWER KEY

Page 1 1. running 2. shortest kind of running events 3. the run 4. throwing and jumping contests 5. jumping the greatest distance forward after a running start 6. a raised bar 7. discus 8. heavy metal ball
Extended Activity: a race over a distance of 26 miles 385 yards

Page 2 1. scientists not sure where it came from 2. big iron core 3. predictable-able to tell what will happen; wobble-to move, sway, or shake; core-the central part of something; mystery-something not known or understood; steady-not changing; constant; even; tilt-slant; lean; slope 4. about four and a half billion years ago 5. it is tilted 6. could not grow food - Answers may vary.   Extended Activity: water, oxygen, clouds, living creatures, magnetic field

Page 3 I. A. 1. Warm-blooded B. Fish 1. cold-blooded II. A. Whales B. Fish 1. Vertical III. Breathing A. Whales B. Fish 1. Gills IV. A. 1. Live birth B. Fish 1. Lay eggs   Extended Activity: The female nurses its young.

Page 4 aardvark, armadillo, tapir 1. tapir 2. Africa 3. horse and rhinoceros, 4. protection from attack by other animals
Extended Activity: Reports will vary.

Page 5 5, 2, 7, 1, 4, 8, 3, 6, 9   Extended Activity: god of the sea and of horses

Page 6 1. auricle 2. anvil 3. hammer 4. cochlea 5. canal 6. stirrup 7. eardrum
Extended Activity: sight, hearing, smell, taste, touch

Page 7 1. 45 2. [maze drawing] 3. Susan, 14; Benjamin, 14; James, 13; Alan, 13; Patricia, 15   Extended Activity: [arrow diagrams]

Page 8 1. the kind of cloud in which they form 2. tall, cumulous clouds; thunderheads 3. horizontal, layered clouds 4. turbulence 5. air pressure 6. are heavier and can cut through the atmosphere better
Extended Activity: cirrus clouds, form above 20,000 feet

Page 9 1. b. 2. a. 3. c. 4. b. 5. c.   Extended Activity: Northwest: Idaho, Washington, Oregon

Page 10 1. famous explorers 2. places and cultures around the world 3. Feb. 20, 1995 4. Australia, London, Rome, Poland, Puerto Rico 5. to hold mementos for the students   Extended Activity: Pike-discovered Pike's Peak; Drake-sailed around the world; Hudson-explored the waters of northeast North America; Louis & Clark-explored the Northwest; Hillary-first person to climb Mount Everest

Page 11 1. he was shipwrecked 2. 30 years 3. pelicans 4. scientific societies 5. wax models 6. 1890's 7. Answers will vary.
Extended Activity: Answers will vary.

Page 12 1. False 2. True 3. True 4. False 5. False THREE   Extended Activity: first person to step on the moon

Page 13 1. b. 2. 3rd 3. temperature 4. controls body temperature 5. false 6. harm brain cells 7. becomes, sometimes, itself, something, inside, into, bloodstream, overcome   Extended Activity: Answers will vary.

Page 14 I. A. Dead-leaf mantis B. Bittern 1. Looks like a reed C. Pipefish 1. Looks like a plant II. Animals with special coloring A. White-tailed fawn 1. Spotted B. Polar bear. 1. White coat C. Tiger 1. Stripes
Extended Activity: Answers will vary.

Page 15 1. False 2. True 3. False 4. True 5. True HOUSE   Extended Activity: Answers will vary.

Page 16 1. In size, it is a little smaller than the state of Kentucky. 2. Boiling water from geysers is piped to cities to heat buildings. 3. mild 4. Winds blowing across the warm currents keep the average winter temperature at about 32°F. 5. Its northern point touches the Arctic Circle. 6. 32, 50 7. 200   Extended Activity: Answers will vary.

Page 17 1. library in Philadelphia 2. College of Pennsylvania 3. independence 4. Postmaster General 5. France 6. October 25, 1770   Extended Activity: Letters will vary.

Page 18 1. audience 2. talking pictures 3. *The Jazz Singer*, Al Jolsen 4. actors, actor, big star, big star, voice, movie-goers
Extended Activity: actions told the story; subtitles were printed on the screen. Answers will vary.

Page 19 1. eastern California 2. lowest, driest, hottest 3. people traveling from the East to California during the 1849 Gold Rush 4. someone who lives through a life-threatening situation 5. many people died there trying to cross it 6. the amount of rain falling in one year 7. roads, water, and hotels are there
Extended Activity: 14,496 feet

Page 20 1. have it examined by experts 2. ask for identification, or ask for cash instead of a check 3. He felt if he could make another identical statue, it would prove he had made the first one.
Extended Activity: to take someone else's ideas or writings and pass them off as your own

Page 21 Top clockwise: sentry tower, living spaces, courtyard, pennant, lookout, keep, moat, slits, outer walls, drawbridge
Extended Activity: from 400's to 1500's

Page 22 congregate, terminates, pachyderm, protrude, elderly, carnivore, solitary, superb Differences: size, ears, back, trunks, color Similarities: food, herds, eyesight, sense of smell, age   Extended Activity: Answers will vary.

Page 23 German hikers, CAT scans and X-rays, 1991, at a radiology meeting in Chicago, many serious injuries were found on the corpse   Extended Activity: computerized axial tomography shows disorders of the soft tissue of a body

Page 24 1. acid rain 2. contaminates it 3. sulfur dioxide 4. carries polluted air miles away 5. automobile engines 6. they mix with clouds 7. rain, snow 8. moves contaminated water to other places
Extended Activity: Answers will vary.

Page 25 1. The official name of the Rough Riders was the First United States Volunteer Cavalry. 2. Cuba 3. Lieutenant Colonel 4. They were buffalo hunters, Indian fighters, cowboys, gamblers, churchmen, and daring adventurers. 5. The Spanish were defeated. 6. good shots 7. President of the United States   Extended Activity: A large island in the West Indies; south of Florida

Page 26 1. Japan 2. Iwo Jima 3. Navajo Indians 4. Navajo's language 5. Japanese could not break their coded messages. 6. figure out what the code means 7. enemy would not know what plans were being made against them
Extended Activity: This way of talking is called pig Latin.

Page 27 1. wee, mischievous, little, playful, impish 2. wee 3. unfortunately 4. take the money 5. lucky 6. outside 7. where 8. landmarks   Extended Activity: They are imaginary beings told about in legends.

Page 28 1. five 2. Atlantic 3. four 4. He didn't find the route to India. 5. disgraced 6. Spain 7. King Ferdinand
Extended Activity: Italian

Page 29 extract, research, ability, venom, poisonous, murky, clot, stalks, bait, antidote, prey, rabid
Extended Activity: Answers will vary.

Page 30 1. Thailand 2. China 3. centuries 4. banquet 5. one-time royal seat, 6. fruits, vegetables, boiled eggs, nuts, and sweets 7. enthusiasm   Extended Activity: Asia

Comprehension Collection 6   ©Remedia Publications 1995

Name_____

WHALES AND FISH

Whales look very much like fish, but they are different from fish. Although both live only in water, the two have little else in common.

A whale is a warm-blooded being, which means its body temperature is always about the same. A fish is cold-blooded. Its body temperature changes as the temperature of the water changes.

Whales have horizontal tail fins. They spread from side to side. Fish have vertical tail fins that are lengthwise with their bodies.

Whales are air-breathing. They must come to the surface of the water to take in oxygen. Fish get oxygen from the water through their gills.

Fish lay eggs from which the babies hatch. Whales give birth to live babies.

Complete the outline with details from the story.

WHALES AND FISH

I. Body temperature
  A. Whales
      1. _____
  B. _____
      1. _____

II. Tail fins
  A. _____
      1. Horizontal
  B. _____
      1. _____

III. _____
  A. _____
      1. Air-breathing
  B. _____
      1. _____

IV. Producing young
  A. Whales
      1. _____
  B. _____
      1. _____

EXTENDED ACTIVITY: Whales are mammals. What does this mean?

©Remedia Publications 1995   3   Comprehension Collection 6

Name_____

WHAT ANIMAL AM I?

Read each description; then write the animal's name under its picture.

         aardvark   tapir   armadillo

    I look like I should belong to the pig family but, actually, I am related to the horse and rhinoceros. I am most active at night and I love very warm climates.

    I have strong claws which I use to dig into nests of ants or termites. I use my long, sticky tongue to capture them. I live in Africa. I have no front teeth.

    My body is covered with strong plates which are made of bone. These plates protect me from attack by other animals. I eat insects.

_____   _____   _____

1. Which animal would be very unhappy in a cold climate?
   _____

2. On what continent would you find an aardvark?_____

3. The tapir is related to what other animals?_____

4. Why is an armadillo's body covered with plates?_____
   _____

EXTENDED ACTIVITY: Choose one of the above animals. Write a short report about the animal.

Comprehension Collection 6   4   ©Remedia Publications 1995

Name_____

USING LOGIC

1. One day, Lisa got into her car and began the fifteen-mile drive to her job. Half way there, she realized that she had forgotten her briefcase. She returned home to get it. Lisa was 20 minutes late to work. How many miles did she travel to and from work that day?_____

2. Use a crayon or marker to draw a continuous line from START to END. Do not lift the marker from the paper; do not draw along any line twice; do not cross a line.

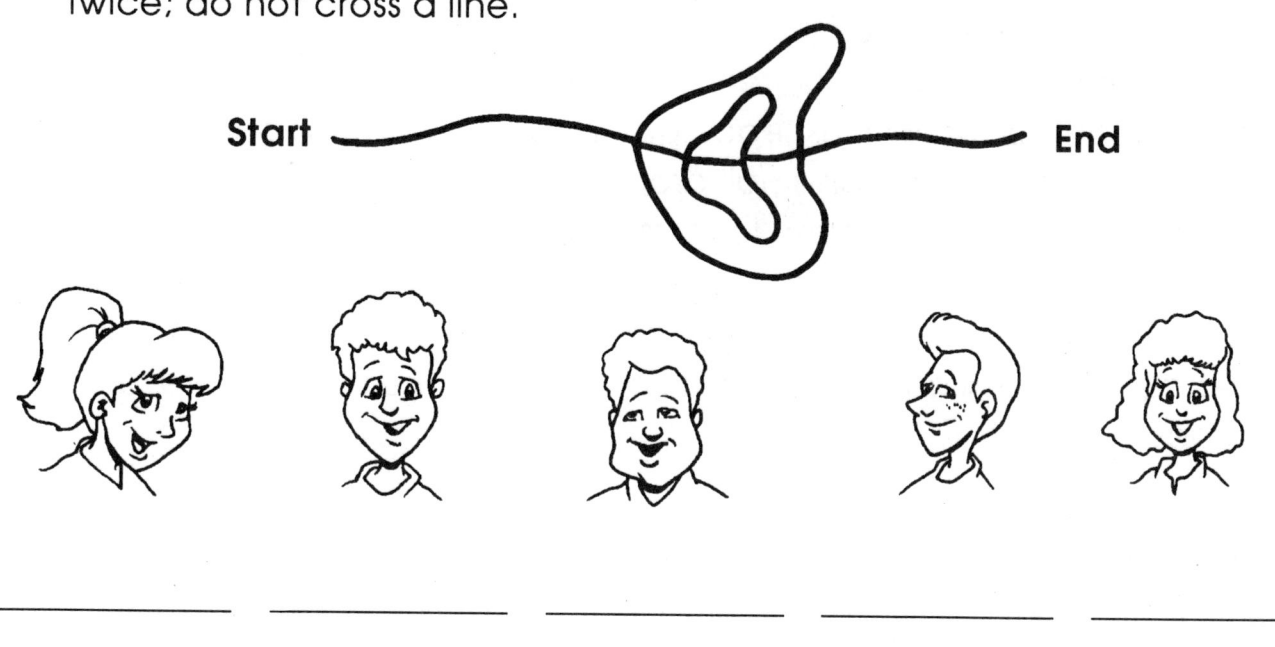

   Start ———————————————— End

   _____   _____   _____   _____   _____

   _____   _____   _____   _____   _____

3. Read the clues, then write the names under the pictures.

   >Alan is between Patricia and James.
   >Susan is to the left of Benjamin.

   Read the clues, then write the ages under the names.

   >Pat is two years older than Jim.
   >Ben is one year younger than Pat.
   >Al is the same age as Jim, who just became a teenager.
   >Sue and Ben are twins.

EXTENDED ACTIVITY: Decide which pattern comes next in the row. Draw six more patterns.

Name_____

Why are raindrops different sizes?

Sometimes raindrops are heavy, fat drops that splat down hard against a window. Other times fine, small drops seem to fall lightly. The difference in size is caused by the kinds of clouds in which they form.

Big, fat raindrops usually come from thunderheads, those tall cumulus clouds common in summer. The wind currents force the droplets up and down against each other and they grow bigger and bigger. The big drops fall faster than small drops.

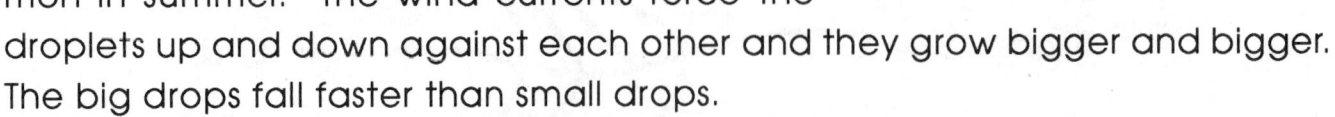

The smaller raindrops tend to form in horizontal, layered clouds. There is much less turbulence in these clouds so the drops are not forced together into larger drops. Small raindrops cannot fall as fast as large drops. Air pressure pushes against them and they cannot cut through the atmosphere as well as big drops.

1. What causes different sized raindrops?_____
   _____

2. Big, fat raindrops come from what kind of clouds?_____
   _____

3. In what kind of clouds do small raindrops form?_____
   _____

4. What word in paragraph 3 means strong movement, such as violent wind?_____

5. What keeps small raindrops from falling fast?_____

6. Why can big drops fall faster than the small ones?_____
   _____

EXTENDED ACTIVITY: What is the name given to clouds that form at the highest elevations? How high up are they? Use an encyclopedia or dictionary to find the answers.

Comprehension Collection 6 ©Remedia Publications 1995

Name_____

SPECIAL HORSES

When Spanish explorers came to America many years ago, they brought horses with them. Some of those horses were oddly marked with brown or black spots.

The Nez Perce Indians liked these spotted horses. They traded goods for them whenever they could. The horses were called appaloosas.

The appaloosas were swift runners. Buffaloes could also run very fast. The Indians could overtake a running buffalo easily when riding an appaloosa.

Later, the Nez Perce Indians were moved to a reservation. There were no more buffaloes to hunt. Their herds of appaloosas grew smaller, until only a few of them were left.

Luckily, some people realized that appaloosas would be good animals for herding cows. They built up the breed again. Now there are thousands of appaloosas in America.

Circle the letter of the correct answer.

1. This story is mainly about
   a. Nez Perce Indians   b. horses   c. buffaloes

2. The main idea of paragraph three is to tell about
   a. the horse's speed   b. chasing buffaloes   c. how Indians rode horses

3. The main idea of paragraph four is to tell about
   a. buffalo hunting   b. the Nez Perce moving   c. how appaloosas almost disappeared

4. The paragraph that tells how appaloosas came to America is
   a. paragraph five   b. paragraph one   c. paragraph two

5. This story tells about the history of the
   a. Nez Perce   b. Spanish explorers   c. appaloosas

EXTENDED ACTIVITY: Read about the Nez Perce Indians in an encyclopedia or dictionary. In what part of the United States did they live?

Name_____

NEVADA STAR

Kids See the World Through Eyes of Bears

(Las Vegas, February 20, 1995) - Students in many schools across the country are combining a fun research project with their geography lessons. They are learning about places and cultures around the world through the eyes of traveling toy bears.

The bears are called Geobears. Each bear wears a name tag with instructions on where to send pictures or postcards telling about the bear's travels. They also carry small backpacks to hold mementos for the students when they finally return home.

Companies and individuals volunteer to carry the bears on business trips or vacations to faraway places.

Five Geobears are now traveling for an eighth-grade class at Henderson Jr. High School. The bears are named for famous explorers. Zeb is named for Zebulon Pike, Frank for Sir Francis Drake, Hank for Henry Hudson, Louie for Lewis and Clark, and Eddie for Sir Edmund Hillary.

Postcards and pictures have been sent from Australia, London, Rome, Poland, Puerto Rico, and many other places. The students keep track of their bears' journeys by putting push-pins on a world map.

1. <u>Who</u> are Geobears named for?_____
2. <u>What</u> do students learn about from the bears?_____
   _____
3. <u>When</u> did this story appear in the newspaper?_____
4. <u>Where</u> have the Geobears been traveling?
   _____
5. <u>Why</u> do the bears carry backpacks?_____
   _____

EXTENDED ACTIVITY: Look up the names of the explorers in an encyclopedia or dictionary. Write what each one is famous for.

Comprehension Collection 6 ©Remedia Publications 1995

Name_____

THE WORLD'S GREATEST LIAR

Sometimes people can be so convincing in the way they tell stories that everyone believes them. This happened in England in the 1890's.

Louis de Rougement caused a sensation when he wrote an article for *Wide World* magazine. The story described his 30 years of living among the cannibals of Australia. He said he had been shipwrecked there. He told about taking part in cannibal feasts, that he built a house of pearl shells, and that he rode on 600-pound turtles. He claimed he sent off fleets of pelicans carrying messages in six languages. He once cured himself of a fever by sleeping in the body of a dead buffalo.

So convincing was his account that scientific societies invited him to give lectures about his experiences. A waxworks model of him was placed in Madam Tussaud's in London.

After finally being exposed as a fraud, Louis cashed in again by giving speeches on his great deception. He described himself as "The Greatest Liar on Earth," and people wanted to hear about that, too!

1. How did Louis land on Australia?_____

2. How long did he say he lived there?_____

3. What carried messages for him?_____

4. Who invited him to lecture about his experiences?_____
   _____

5. Madam Tussaud's displayed what kind of models of famous people?
   _____

6. When did de Rougement's hoax take place?_____

7. Do you think Louis was embarrassed when he was exposed as a fraud?
   _____ Why or why not?_____
   _____

EXTENDED ACTIVITY: Write an article describing a fantastic, but untrue, experience you had. Be convincing!

©Remedia Publications 1995   11   Comprehension Collection 6

Name_____

JOHN GLENN'S BOYHOOD

On February 20, 1962, Colonel John H. Glenn, Jr., became America's first astronaut to circle the earth in a space capsule called Friendship 7. He always will be remembered for that historic flight.

John Glenn, Jr., was born in Columbus, Ohio, in 1921. Two years later, his family moved to the nearby town of New Concord. His father owned a plumbing and heating business there.

Even as a child, John was interested in aviation. He made balsa wood models of airplanes. He had a collection of pictures of famous flyers and their planes. He liked to read about heroes in aviation.

In high school, John played a trumpet in the band. He helped form an organization called the Ohio Rangers. The Rangers built a cabin where they spent weekends. They fished, hiked, and hunted rabbits.

When John was a young man, he married Anna Castor, a girl he had known and loved since his high-school days.

If the statement is true, circle the letter in the TRUE column. If it is not true, circle the letter in the FALSE column.

		TRUE	FALSE
1.	John was born in New Concord, Ohio.	M	T
2.	John's father was named John Glenn.	H	S
3.	Aviation was an interest of John's at an early age.	R	B
4.	The Ohio Rangers were a group of pilots.	A	E
5.	John married a girl he met at college.	W	E

Write the letters you circled on the lines to complete the sentence.

John Glenn orbited the earth ___ ___ ___ ___ ___ times during his first space flight.

EXTENDED ACTIVITY: Another astronaut, Neil Armstrong, also accomplished a "first." What did he do? Use an encyclopedia or dictionary to find the answer.

Name_____

HEATING UP

A person who becomes sick may get a fever. A fever happens when the temperature of the body rises above normal. In a healthy person, the body temperature is about 98.6 degrees. With a fever, it could reach 101 or 103 degrees, sometimes even higher.

A fever is not a sickness in itself, but is a sign that something else is wrong. When a person is ill, germs inside the body make poisons. These poisons get into the bloodstream and travel to the brain. The brain has a thermostat that controls body temperature. When the poisons reach this point, the body heats up.

Not only is a fever a sign of illness, but it is also nature's way of fighting the illness. The fever helps to overcome the infection.

An overly high fever can be dangerous. It can harm brain cells. The person is very sick and should be cared for by a doctor.

Once the poison-causing germs in the body die, the fever will leave and the temperature will return to normal.

1. Underline the correct answer. The main idea of paragraph one is that a. people get sick, b. body temperature rises with a fever, c. normal body temperature is 98.6 degrees.
2. Which paragraph tells about the good thing a fever does?_____
3. What word means "degree of hotness or coldness of something"?
   _____
4. The brain's thermostat does what?_____
5. True or false? A fever is a sickness. _____
6. Overly high fevers can do what?_____
7. Write all the compound words in the article._____
   _____

EXTENDED ACTIVITY: Name three illnesses that may cause a fever.

©Remedia Publications 1995   13   Comprehension Collection 6

Name_____

ANIMALS WITH SPECIAL DEFENSES

Many animals could not survive if it were not for the special defenses they have against their enemies. Some animals have special shapes that are like the shapes found in their natural surroundings. The dead-leaf mantis could easily be mistaken for a leaf while it is resting on a branch. The long-necked, slender bittern, a water bird, looks like a reed when standing among the reeds. The pipefish has a long body shaped like an underwater plant.

The special coloring of some animals helps keep them hidden from their enemies. The fawn of the white-tailed deer is spotted in a way that makes it difficult to see in the forest where it lives. The white coat of the polar bear makes it hard to see in the snow. When a tiger stands in tall grass, its stripes keep it well hidden from other animals. Animals with special coloring usually do not move until the danger has passed.

Complete the outline.

ANIMALS WITH SPECIAL DEFENSES

I. Animals with special shapes
    A. _____
        1. Looks like a leaf
    B. _____
        1. _____
    C. _____
        1. _____

II. _____
    A. _____
        1. _____
    B. _____
        1. _____
    C. _____
        1. _____

EXTENDED ACTIVITY: Name another animal whose shape is a special defense and tell why. Name another animal whose color is a special defense and tell why.

Name_____

Benjamin Franklin was a famous American who was a statesman, a printer, a publisher, an inventor, and a scientist. In this letter from his brother, James, you learn more about his many interests.

> Philadelphia
> October 25, 1770
>
> Dear Ben,
>
> When I visited the library in Philadelphia today, I thought of you at once. If you hadn't promoted the idea of a public library, I would not have been able to get the book I wanted to read! Also, thanks to you, the Academy of Philadelphia is now the College of Pennsylvania where my son, Clarence, will be a student next spring.
>
> How you have helped to improve our lives here in the colonies! I have heard that you are in favor of independence. Is that true? I wonder what will come of these ideas?
>
> Now that you are Postmaster General, what do you have to do? Do you have time to travel? Do you still want to spend time in France someday?
>
> Come and visit us when you are able.
>
> Your brother,
> James

1. Where did James get the book he wanted?_____

2. Where will Clarence be a student next spring?_____
   _____

3. What idea about the colonies does Benjamin Franklin favor?
   _____

4. What job does Benjamin Franklin have at the time of this letter?
   _____

5. Where does Benjamin Franklin hope to spend time someday?
   _____

6. When did James write the letter?_____

EXTENDED ACTIVITY: Pretend you are Benjamin Franklin. Write a letter to your brother James. Tell about one of your (Ben's) inventions. Use an encyclopedia for information.

©Remedia Publications 1995   Comprehension Collection 6

Name_____

TALKING PICTURES

In 1907, in a Cleveland, Ohio, movie theater, the audience stared in wonder. On the screen a bullfight was being shown, and they could actually hear the snorts of the bull! These people were viewing the very first talking pictures shown in the United States.

Since then, talking pictures have changed and improved. In 1926, they reached the form in which they are now shown.

In 1927, the movie *The Jazz Singer* was made. It starred Al Jolsen and was a smashing success. People all over the United States became fans of his as well as devoted movie-goers.

Not all actors were happy about talking pictures. Some found themselves out of work. One was a big star on the silent screen. He had played many dashing, romantic roles. Audiences had never heard his voice, which was high-pitched and shrill. It did not go with his handsome, manly face. Movie-goers didn't like it, and they stopped going to that actor's films.

1. In the first paragraph, what does *they* refer to?_____
2. What are *they* in the second paragraph?_____
3. In paragraph three, what is *It*?_____
   Who does *his* refer to?_____
4. Tell what the following words refer to in the last paragraph.

   Some _____

   One   _____

   He   _____

   his   _____

   It   _____

   They _____

EXTENDED ACTIVITY: Write a paragraph answering this question: How do you think an audience knew what was happening in a silent movie?

Comprehension Collection 6   ©Remedia Publications 1995

Name_____

DEATH VALLEY

The lowest point of land in the United States is a desert valley in eastern California. It is also the driest and hottest spot in America. The annual rainfall is about three inches and summer temperatures of 134° have been recorded there. The valley is 280 feet below sea level. It is about 130 miles long and lies in a dry river bed between high mountains.

The name, Death Valley, was given to the area by a survivor of a group of "forty-niners," most of whom died of thirst in the sands trying to cross the valley. The forty-niners were people traveling from the East to California during the 1849 Gold Rush.

While Death Valley killed many travelers in the past, today it is a popular tourist site. Good roads have been built, water is piped in, and hotels are there. Visitors enjoy seeing this strange, barren land, so different from the places where they live.

1. Where is Death Valley?_____
2. It is the _____, the _____, and the _____ spot in the United States.
3. Who were the "forty-niners"?_____
   _____
4. What is a survivor?_____
   _____
5. Why is it called Death Valley?_____
   _____
6. What does "annual rainfall" mean?_____
   _____
7. Why is it safe to go to Death Valley now?_____
   _____

EXTENDED ACTIVITY: Death Valley is 86 miles east of Mt. Whitney, the highest peak in the U.S. except Alaska. How high is Mt. Whitney?

Name_____

DON'T BE FOOLED

Sometimes people try to pass off something as being real or original when in fact it is a fake. This is called forgery, and it is a crime. Making copies of something is not wrong as long as the copier does not claim it is an original or true.

Signing someone else's name to a check or other document and claiming to be that person is forgery.

Forgery sometimes happens with great works of art. Some forgeries are so good that a team of experts must examine the artwork. They will study samples of the paint and carefully check the frame and signature to determine if they are genuine.

One time an artist in Mexico was arrested and charged with stealing a priceless statue from an ancient tomb. He had made a copy that was so good, even experts thought it was authentic. In prison, the man asked for clay, and he made another statue just like the one he was accused of stealing. The man was set free.

1. Someone claims to have found a long-lost, valuable work of art and is willing to sell it to you for much less than it is worth. What is the logical thing to do?

_____

2. You sell something to a stranger. The person writes you a check in payment. What is the logical thing to do?

_____

3. How did the artist in the story use logic to prove he had not stolen the statue?

_____

EXTENDED ACTIVITY: Find *plagiarize* in a dictionary. What does it mean?

Name_____

CASTLES

People visiting Europe today enjoy seeing castles from the past. Castles were the homes and forts of noblemen during the Middle Ages.

The **outer walls** of the castle were thick and strong. There were **slits** in the walls for shooting arrows at enemies. Around the outside of the castle wall was a large ditch called a **moat**. It was filled with water to help keep invaders away.

The castle entrance was protected by a **drawbridge** which could be pulled up at night or during battles. A guard watched over the entrance from a small, round **sentry tower** at the front corner of the castle.

The tall, square tower in the center of the castle was called the **keep**. The lord of the castle lived there. Servants had **living spaces** around a **courtyard** in the middle of the castle.

The tallest tower, or **lookout**, had small windows from which the whole countryside could be seen. It was topped by the lord's flag, or **pennant**.

Label the parts of the castle.

EXTENDED ACTIVITY: What period of history is known as the Middle Ages? Use a dictionary or encyclopedia to find the dates.

Name_____

ELEPHANTS

There are two kinds of elephants, the African elephant and the Asian elephant. The larger of the two, the African elephant, has huge, fan-shaped ears that protrude from its head. It has a long, straight back, and its trunk terminates in two lips. It is dark gray in color.

The Asian elephant has ears that are smaller than the African pachyderm, and they are pressed back against its body. It has a rounded back and a solitary lip at the end of its trunk. Most Asian elephants are light gray.

Neither kind is a carnivore. Both live mostly on leaves, roots and grasses. They usually congregate in large groups called herds. All elephants have poor eyesight but a superb sense of smell. Both African and Asian elephants live to be quite elderly, usually about sixty years. Some reach an age of more than one hundred years.

Write each underlined word next to its definition.

_____ gather; come together
_____ ends
_____ elephant
_____ stand out; stick out
_____ old
_____ meat-eater
_____ one; single
_____ very good; excellent

List the ways in which the elephants are different and the ways in which they are the same.

DIFFERENCES	SIMILARITIES
_____	_____
_____	_____
_____	_____
_____	_____
_____	_____

EXTENDED ACTIVITY: It has been said that elephants are afraid of mice. Do you think this is true? Write a paragraph giving your answer and reasons why you have that opinion.

Comprehension Collection 6   ©Remedia Publications 1995

Name_____

THE DAILY NEWS

Ice Man May Have Been a Fugitive

(Chicago, December 7, 1994) - Scientists from Innsbruck, Austria, came here to present a report at a radiology meeting about their latest findings on "Ice Man." Ice Man is 5,300 years old. His nearly perfect remains were discovered on an Alpine glacier in 1991.

Researchers now think he may have been a beaten and bloody fugitive who died in hiding while others searched for him.

Through the use of Space Age CAT scans and X-rays, many serious injuries were found on the Stone Age corpse. It is thought that he was trying to escape from enemies who had already beaten him.

He hid in a hollow high in the mountains. After falling asleep, he soon froze to death. A snowfall buried him and gradually the site was covered by a glacier.

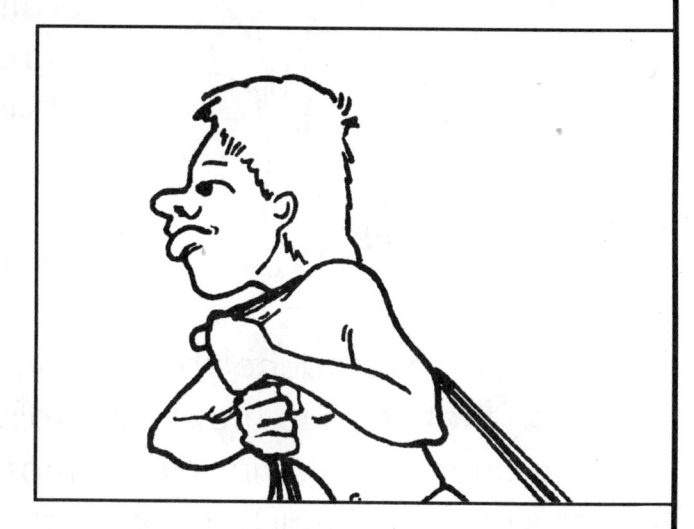

Over 5,000 years later, the frozen body came out of the melting glacier. It was found by German hikers.

Ice Man is kept in a special, glacier-like chamber to preserve him for further scientific study.

Who found Ice Man?_____

What did scientists use to examine the body?_____

When was the frozen body discovered?_____

Where was a report on the latest findings presented?_____

_____

Why do researchers think Ice Man was a fugitive?_____

_____

EXTENDED ACTIVITY: Find CAT scan in a dictionary. What do the letters CAT stand for? What does a CAT scan show?

Name_____

ACID RAIN

Acid rain is the term used to describe a type of pollution when rain, snow, hail, or fog contain sulfuric and nitric acids. Acid rain has destroyed plant and animal life in lakes. It has harmed forests and crops, contaminated drinking water, and even damaged buildings.

Acid rain forms when sulfur dioxide is released into the air during the burning of oil and coal. Nitrogen oxides produced by automobile engines are another major source of pollution that helps to make acid rain.

The chemicals rise into the atmosphere. They mix with clouds. Then the harmful chemicals fall back to earth in rain or snow.

Winds can carry the air miles away from where it was polluted, causing widespread damage from acid rain. Rivers move water contaminated by acid rain to other places. Acid rain has become a world-wide problem.

1. Air containing certain chemicals causes what?_____

2. What is the effect of acid rain on drinking water?_____

3. Name the chemical that is caused by burning oil and coal.
   _____

4. Wind has what effect on acid rain?_____
   _____

5. What is the cause of nitrogen oxide in the air?_____

6. What is the effect when chemicals rise into the atmosphere?
   _____

7. What causes the acids to fall back to earth?_____
   _____

8. How do rivers cause the problem to spread?_____
   _____

EXTENDED ACTIVITY: Write two examples of cause and effect.

Comprehension Collection 6

Name_____

ROUGH RIDERS

During the Spanish-American War of 1898, the Rough Riders became a famous group of soldiers. They served under the command of Teddy Roosevelt. The official name of the Rough Riders was the First United States Volunteer Cavalry.

A thousand men were hand-picked for the Rough Riders. These men were "good shots and good riders." They were buffalo hunters, Indian fighters, cowboys, gamblers, churchmen, and daring adventurers.

At the Battle of San Juan Hill in Cuba, the Rough Riders had their greatest victory. The troops were near a hill above the San Juan River where Spanish soldiers were stationed. Lieutenant Colonel Theodore Roosevelt led the charge up the hill. Under heavy fire by the enemy, the Rough Riders took San Juan Hill. The Spanish were defeated.

Teddy Roosevelt became an American hero. He was admired for his bravery. Later, Theodore Roosevelt was elected President of the United States.

Follow the directions.

1. Underline the sentence that shows the name Rough Riders was a nickname.
2. Put an X on the word that tells where the Battle of San Juan Hill was fought.
3. Put parentheses around Roosevelt's official rank in the army.
4. Write the sentence that describes who the men were that were chosen to be Rough Riders.

_____

_____

5. Circle the sentence that tells what happened to the enemy.
6. Draw a line through the words that mean the Rough Riders were fine marksmen.
7. Write the five words that tell what Theodore Roosevelt became later in life.

_____

EXTENDED ACTIVITY: Describe what the land of Cuba is and where it is located. Use a dictionary, encyclopedia, or atlas to find the information.

Name_____

CODE TALKERS

During World War II, United States soldiers from the Navajo Indian tribe used their own language as a secret weapon against the Japanese. This secret weapon has been credited with shortening the war in the Pacific.

Commanders in all wars use secret codes to send messages to each other. Often, the messages are heard by the enemy. Experts are able to break the codes and the enemy can then learn what plans are being made against them.

The language of the Navajo is very different from any other language. The Navajo soldiers who sent and received coded messages in their own language were called code talkers. Even though the Japanese were still able to hear the messages, they were never able to break the code of the Navajo code talkers.

Marines fighting in Iwo Jima and other islands in the Pacific were grateful for the help of the 400 Native Americans. The secret weapon of the Navajo code talkers saved many lives and helped to hasten the end of the war.

1. The United States was in a war with what country?_____
2. What island is named in the story?_____
3. Who were the code talkers?_____
4. What was the secret weapon?_____
5. Why was the secret weapon so helpful during the war?_____
   _____
6. What does "break the code" mean?_____
   _____
7. How would an unbreakable code help to hasten the end of the war?
   _____

EXTENDED ACTIVITY: Can you break this code? Is thay   a way   of a auking tay   is a   alled cay   ig pay   atin Lay.

Comprehension Collection 6   26   ©Remedia Publications 1995

Name_____

MEDICINE MAN

There is a man in Texas, Terry Fredeking, who makes his living hunting <u>poisonous</u> creatures. He does not hunt to kill but to capture them alive.

Crawling on his elbows and knees and armed with a flashlight and a jar, the hunter searches at night for black widow spiders. Fredeking also hunts for scorpions, diamondback rattlesnakes, and Brazilian pit vipers. He <u>stalks</u> <u>rabid</u> vampire bats to <u>extract</u> their saliva with an eyedropper. He has collected six-inch-long Mexican leeches by wading through <u>murky</u> waters, using his own legs as <u>bait</u>.

All of this hunting is done to help scientists in their <u>research</u> for new kinds of medicine. Black widow poison is used to make an <u>antidote</u> for victims of the spider's bite. Snake <u>venom</u> has led to the development of drugs to treat high blood pressure. Leeches have the <u>ability</u> to cause blood to <u>clot</u> and researchers want to know how they do it.

Terry Fredeking enjoys the excitement of hunting dangerous <u>prey</u>, and he also likes knowing that he is helping medical research.

Write each underlined word next to its definition.

_____ to take out or pull out
_____ a careful investigation or study of something
_____ the power or skill to do something
_____ poison that can be given through a bite or sting
_____ causing harm or death by poison
_____ dark, cloudy, dirty
_____ to make thick or form into soft lumps
_____ moves in a quiet, cautious way
_____ something that attracts or lures an animal or fish
_____ a medicine that stops the effect of a poison
_____ an animal that is the target of a hunter
_____ having rabies, a disease of the central nervous system

EXTENDED ACTIVITY: Would you like to do the kind of work Terry Fredeking does? Write a paragraph giving reasons for your answer.

Name_____

GOOD MONKEY BUSINESS

In the town of Lopburi, Thailand, thousands of monkeys stroll on the sidewalks, relax on people's balconies, and walk into food stores hoping that generous shopkeepers will feed them. Monkeys have been residents of this one-time royal seat for centuries.

The people in Lopburi believe that the monkeys bring good luck to those who treat them kindly. Yongyuth Kitwatananusont, who was a poor Chinese immigrant, believes the monkeys are responsible for his good fortune. After moving to Lopburi, he became a very wealthy businessman.

Every year, Yongyuth gives thanks to the monkeys by providing them with a special feast. Troops of monkeys descend on huge tables covered by red tablecloths. On them is a bounty of fruits, vegetables, boiled eggs, nuts, and sweets. The latest banquet cost $50,000, but Yongyuth didn't complain. "If I pay respect to the monkeys, business always turns out very good," he said with enthusiasm.

1. In what country is Lopburi?_____
2. Yongyuth Kitwatananusont was an immigrant from what country?
   _____
3. How long have monkeys been living in Lopburi?_____
4. What other word in the story means the same as feast?
   _____
5. What phrase states that kings and queens probably lived in Lopburi in the past?_____
6. What kind of food was served at the banquet?_____
   _____
7. Which word tells how Yongyuth expressed his opinion about the cost of the food?_____

EXTENDED ACTIVITY: Find *Thailand* in an encyclopedia or dictionary. On what continent is it located?

Comprehension Collection 6   30   ©Remedia Publications 1995